Descendants of George Schmeiser

Generation 1

1. **GEORGE[1] SCHMEISER** was born on 15 Jun 1721 in Wurtenburg, Germany. He died in 1747 in York County, Pennsylvania. He married Maria Barbara Stambaugh, daughter of Jacob Stambaugh and Mary Elizabeth (unknown) on 22 May 1740 in York County, Pennsylvania. She was born about 1720 in Germany. She died about 1800.

   Notes for George Schmeiser:
   Came to America in 1731.

   George Schmeiser and Maria Barbara Stambaugh had the following children:

   2.   i. **MATHIAS[2] SMYSER** was born in 1742 in York County, Pennsylvania. He died in 1780 in Washington County, Maryland. He married Anna Angela Linebacker, daughter of Henry Linebacker and Catherine (unknown) in 1763 in York County, Pennsylvania. She was born about 1742 in York County, Pennsylvania. She died about 1835 in Jefferson County, Kentucky.

         ii. JOHN MICHAEL SMYSER was born on 17 Jul 1743 in York County, Pennsylvania.

        iii. JOHN JACOB SMYSER was born on 19 Mar 1747 in York County, Pennsylvania.

Generation 2

2. **MATHIAS[2] SMYSER** (George[1] Schmeiser) was born in 1742 in York County, Pennsylvania. He died in 1780 in Washington County, Maryland. He married Anna Angela Linebacker, daughter of Henry Linebacker and Catherine (unknown) in 1763 in York County, Pennsylvania. She was born about 1742 in York County, Pennsylvania. She died about 1835 in Jefferson County, Kentucky.

   More About Mathias Smyser:
   Military Service: 1776; Militia, Washington County, Maryland

   Notes for Mathias Smyser:
   Enlisted in Bennett's Company, Washington County, Maryland Militia on May 15, 1776.

   Notes for Anna Angela Linebacker:
   Moved to Bourbon County, Kentucky in 1794.

   Mathias Smyser and Anna Angela Linebacker had the following children:

   3.   i. **JOHN[3] SMISER** was born in 1778 in Haggerstown, Maryland. He died in 1848 in Columbia, Maury County, Tennessee. He married Eve Mary Turney, daughter of Daniel Turney and Susan Matheney on 06 Jun 1800 in Bourbon County, Kentucky. She was born on 27 Apr 1780 in Shenandoah County, Virginia. She died on 27 Dec 1844 in Columbia, Maury County, Tennessee.

   4.   ii. HENRY SMISER was born before 08 Apr 1765 in York County, Pennsylvania. He died about 1837 in Oldham County, Kentucky. He married (1) ELIZABETH WEAVER on 10 Oct 1794 in Hagerstown, Maryland. She was born on 14 Nov 1774 in Maryland. She died on 27 Mar 1843 in Indiana. He married (2) JANE FIBLE about 1802 in Oldam County, Kentucky.

   5.   iii. PHILIP SMISER was born in York County, Pennsylvania. He died on 25 Jul 1837 in Milford, Ohio. He married (1) MARY FREY, daughter of John Frey and Margaret (unknown) on 13 Dec 1794 in Bourbon County, Kentucky. She died on 24 Jun 1813 in Clermont County, Ohio. He married (2) MARY CANON about 1815. She was born

in 1792 in Milford, Ohio. She died on 14 Aug 1868 in Milford, Ohio.

6. iv. JACOB SMISER was born on 27 Sep 1768 in Washington County, Maryland. He died on 22 Aug 1829 in Newburgh, Kentucky. He married Nancy Frey, daughter of John Frey and Margaret (unknown) about 1788 in Washington County, Maryland. She was born on 08 Jan 1771 in Washington County, Maryland. She died on 08 Oct 1841 in Newburgh, Kentucky.

7. v. GEORGE SMISER was born on 03 Jun 1769 in York County, Pennsylvania. He died on 22 Apr 1856 in Harrison County, Kentucky. He married (1) CATHERINE LAIR, daughter of Mathias Lair and Ann Rush on 28 Feb 1798 in Bourbon County, Kentucky. She was born on 30 Mar 1778. She died on 27 Jun 1800. He married (2) MARY LAIR, daughter of Mathias Lair and Ann Rush on 05 Dec 1800 in Harrison County, Kentucky. She was born on 06 Aug 1780. She died on 02 Jul 1802. He married (3) MARTHA LAIR, daughter of Andrew Lair and Frances Hubbard on 11 Jan 1803 in Harrison County, Kentucky. She was born on 28 Dec 1780 in Bourbon County, Kentucky. She died on 07 Oct 1857 in Harrison County, Kentucky.

8. vi. MARY MAGDALINE SMISER was born about 1771 in York County, Pennsylvania. She died about 1812 in Jefferson County, Kentucky. She married William Abraham Fry, son of John Frye and Margaret (unknown) on 28 Sep 1794 in Hagerstown, Maryland. He was born about 1770. He died on 13 Sep 1821 in Jefferson County, Kentucky.

9. vii. MICHAEL SMISER was born on 09 Feb 1772 in York County, Pennsylvania. He died on 08 Apr 1855 in Centerfield, Kentucky. He married (1) SALLY OGLESBY on 17 Sep 1797 in Jefferson County, Kentucky. He married (2) ELIZABETH ELLIS on 18 Dec 1804 in Shelby County, Kentucky.

Generation 3

3. JOHN[3] SMISER (Mathias[2] Smyser, George[1] Schmeiser) was born in 1778 in Haggerstown, Maryland. He died in 1848 in Columbia, Maury County, Tennessee. He married Eve Mary Turney, daughter of Daniel Turney and Susan Matheney on 06 Jun 1800 in Bourbon County, Kentucky. She was born on 27 Apr 1780 in Shenandoah County, Virginia. She died on 27 Dec 1844 in Columbia, Maury County, Tennessee.

Notes for John Smiser:
Will dated August 1840.
Built "Fairmont" in Columbia, Tennessee.

John Smiser and Eve Mary Turney had the following children:

10. i. SARAH[4] SMISER was born in 1804. She married JOHN BEIDLER GROVES. He was born on 13 Sep 1797 in Hawkins, Tennessee. He died in Sep 1853 in New Orleans, Louisiana.

11. ii. NANCY W. SMISER was born about 1805 in Maury County, Tennessee. She died before 1840. She married Edward Garland, son of Peter Garland and Mary Reamey on 14 May 1821 in Columbia, Tennessee. He was born before 1807 in Henry County, Virginia. He died before 05 Dec 1850.

12. iii. ELIZA B. SMISER was born about 1809 in Mississippi. She died in 1872. She married Spivey McKissack, son of Thomas McKissack and Lucy Edwards on 31 Oct 1842 in Maury County, Tennessee. He was born on 18 Sep 1790 in North Carolina. He died in 1864 in Columbia, Tennessee.

13. iv. ALFRED SMISER was born about 1811 in Mississippi. He died in May 1865 in Helena, Arkansas. He married Catharine Crockett, daughter of George Crockett and Margaret Adams on 29 Jun 1852 in Davidson, Tennessee. She was born about 1827 in Tennessee.

 v. JOHN SMISER was born about 1813 in Mississippi.

 More About John Smiser:
 Occupation: 1860; Farmer, Planters Township, Arkansas

14. vi. ELLEN MATHENA SMISER was born about 1814. She died in 1892. She married James Gray Booker, son of Peter R. Booker and Susannah Gray on 24 Feb 1835 in Maury County, Tennessee. He was born on 04 Nov 1809 in Williamson County, Tennessee. He died on 19 Aug 1846 in Maury County, Tennessee.

15. vii. JAMES SMISER was born about 1820 in Maury County, Tennessee. He married Charlotte P. Booker on 27 Oct 1847 in Maury County, Tennessee. She was born about 1828 in Virginia.

16. viii. JOSEPH WARREN SMISER was born about 1822 in Tennessee. He died in 1884. He married Martha Page Frierson, daughter of John William Frierson and Lucy Ann Mosby on 23 Dec 1856 in Tennessee. She was born about 1838 in Tennessee.

17. ix. MARIA SMISER was born in 1824. She died on 10 Feb 1849. She married CHARLES L. NELSON.

4. HENRY[3] SMISER (Mathias[2] Smyser, George[1] Schmeiser) was born before 08 Apr 1765 in York County, Pennsylvania. He died about 1837 in Oldham County, Kentucky. He married (1) ELIZABETH WEAVER on 10 Oct 1794 in Hagerstown, Maryland. She was born on 14 Nov 1774 in Maryland. She died on 27 Mar 1843 in Indiana. He married (2) JANE FIBLE about 1802 in Oldam County, Kentucky.

Henry Smiser and Elizabeth Weaver had the following child:
 i. NANCY[4] SMISER was born about 1796 in Kentucky. She married William McDowell on 31 Dec 1817 in Shelby County, Kentucky.

Henry Smiser and Jane Fible had the following children:
 ii. GEORGE MICHAEL SMISER was born on 04 Sep 1802 in Oldham County, Kentucky. He died in Nov 1859 in Lewis County, Missouri.

 iii. JOSEPH SMISER was born about 1804. He died on 11 Nov 1863 in Johnson County, Indiana. He married Elizabeth Deadman on 17 Feb 1825 in Shelby County, Kentucky. She was born on 26 Sep 1797 in Shelby County, Kentucky. She died on 25 Jul 1874 in Johnson County, Indiana.

 iv. JOSHUA O. SMISER was born on 18 Aug 1805 in Oldham County, Kentucky. He died on 23 Sep 1879 in Centerfield, Kentucky.

 v. SAMUEL SMISER was born on 15 Nov 1807 in Oldham County, Kentucky. He died on 29 Jun 1860 in Johnson County, Indiana.

5. PHILIP[3] SMISER (Mathias[2] Smyser, George[1] Schmeiser) was born in York County, Pennsylvania.

He died on 25 Jul 1837 in Milford, Ohio. He married (1) **M ARY FREY**, daughter of John Frey and Margaret (unknown) on 13 Dec 1794 in Bourbon County, Kentucky. She died on 24 Jun 1813 in Clermont County, Ohio. He married (2) **MARY CANON** about 1815. She was born in 1792 in Milford, Ohio. She died on 14 Aug 1868 in Milford, Ohio.

Philip Smiser and Mary Frey had the following children:

    i.   DAVID[4] SMISER was born on 14 Oct 1795 in Harrison County, Kentucky. He died on 21 Jan 1872 in Clermont County, Ohio. He married Ruth Brown, daughter of Joseph Brown and Mary Parker on 13 Oct 1819 in Clermont County, Ohio. She was born on 14 Oct 1802 in Kentucky. She died on 22 May 1854 in Clermont County, Ohio.

        More About David Smiser:
        Burial: Milford, Clermont County, Ohio

    ii.   JOHN SMISER was born on 14 Nov 1799 in Milford, Ohio. He died on 02 May 1868 in Milroy, Indiana.

    iii.   ANNA SMISER was born on 03 Mar 1801 in Milford, Ohio. She died on 22 Jun 1842 in Decatur County, Indiana. She married Daniel Cramer on 03 Apr 1817 in Clermont County, Ohio. He died on 22 Jun 1842 in Decatur County, Indiana.

    iv.   ABRAM SMISER was born on 19 Jan 1804 in Milford, Ohio. He died in Dec 1867 in Milford, Ohio.

    v.   GEORGE SMISER was born on 08 Aug 1808 in Milford, Ohio. He died on 19 Apr 1842 in Clermont County, Ohio. He married Margaret Leming on 16 Feb 1832 in Clermont County, Ohio.

Philip Smiser and Mary Canon had the following children:

    vi.   MARY SMISER was born in 1816 in Milford, Ohio.

    vii.   ELIZABETH SMISER was born in 1817 in Milford, Ohio.

    viii.   PHILLIP SMISER was born in 1819 in Milford, Ohio.

    ix.   HENRY SMISER was born in 1821 in Milford, Ohio.

    x.   JACOB SMISER was born in 1823 in Milford, Ohio.

    xi.   SALLIE SMISER was born in 1825 in Milford, Ohio. She died in 1903 in Sharonville, Ohio.

    xii.   WESLEY SMISER was born on 28 Feb 1828 in Milford, Ohio. He died on 19 Jul 1902 in Sharonville, Ohio.

6.   **JACOB[3] SMISER** (Mathias[2] Smyser, George[1] Schmeiser) was born on 27 Sep 1768 in Washington County, Maryland. He died on 22 Aug 1829 in Newburgh, Kentucky. He married Nancy Frey, daughter of John Frey and Margaret (unknown) about 1788 in Washington County, Maryland. She was born on 08 Jan 1771 in Washington County, Maryland. She died on 08 Oct 1841 in Newburgh, Kentucky.

More About Jacob Smiser:

Occupation: Farmer
Occupation: Blacksmith

Jacob Smiser and Nancy Frey had the following children:

    i.   BETSY[4] SMISER was born about 1788 in Washington County, Maryland. She died on 27 Apr 1838.

    ii.   JACOB SMISER was born on 12 Oct 1792. He died on 27 Oct 1881 in Smyrna, Kentucky.

    iii.   MARY SMISER was born about 1798 in Newburgh, Kentucky.

    iv.   GEORGE SMISER was born on 22 Feb 1799. He died on 31 Dec 1841.

    v.   JOHN WESLEY SMISER was born on 23 Apr 1801. He died in 1853.

    vi.   NANCY SMISER was born about 1805 in Newburgh, Kentucky. She died on 05 Aug 1881. She married William Redding on 29 Sep 1834 in Jefferson County, Kentucky.

    vii.   SALLIE SMISER was born about 1805 in Newburgh, Kentucky. She married Thomas M. Johnson on 16 Sep 1830 in Jefferson County, Kentucky.

    viii.   JOSHUA SMISER was born between 1805-1807 in Oldham County, Kentucky.

    ix.   DELIAH SMISER was born in 1808. She died in 1833.

    x.   WILLIAM JOSEPH SMISER was born on 12 Feb 1809 in Newburgh, Kentucky. He died on 07 Dec 1897 in Ballardsville, Kentucky. He married Sallie Fible, daughter of Joseph Fible and Keziah Wooden on 18 Jan 1831 in Oldham County, Kentucky. She was born on 13 Feb 1813 in Kentucky.

        More About William Joseph Smiser:
        Burial: Fible Cemetery, Oldham County, Kentucky
        Occupation: Farmer
        Occupation: Blacksmith

    xi.   LEWIS SMISER was born in 1811. He died in 1878 in Jefferson County, Kentucky.

7.   GEORGE[3] SMISER (Mathias[2] Smyser, George[1] Schmeiser) was born on 03 Jun 1769 in York County, Pennsylvania. He died on 22 Apr 1856 in Harrison County, Kentucky. He married (1) CATHERINE LAIR, daughter of Mathias Lair and Ann Rush on 28 Feb 1798 in Bourbon County, Kentucky. She was born on 30 Mar 1778. She died on 27 Jun 1800. He married (2) MARY LAIR, daughter of Mathias Lair and Ann Rush on 05 Dec 1800 in Harrison County, Kentucky. She was born on 06 Aug 1780. She died on 02 Jul 1802. He married (3) MARTHA LAIR, daughter of Andrew Lair and Frances Hubbard on 11 Jan 1803 in Harrison County, Kentucky. She was born on 28 Dec 1780 in Bourbon County, Kentucky. She died on 07 Oct 1857 in Harrison County, Kentucky.

Notes for Catherine Lair:

Died during childbirth.

George Smiser and Catherine Lair had the following child:

    i.   ELIZABETH[4] SMISER was born on 20 Jan 1799 in Harrison County, Kentucky. She died on 15 May 1871 in Troy, Ohio.

Notes for Mary Lair:
Died during childbirth, sister of first wife.

Notes for Martha Lair:
Cousin of first and second wife.

George Smiser and Martha Lair had the following children:

ii. SAMUEL MERRIT SMISER was born on 20 Oct 1804 in Harrison County, Kentucky. He died on 23 Feb 1870 in Moultrie County, Illinois.

iii. JOHN MILTON SMISER was born on 02 Feb 1807 in Harrison County, Kentucky. He died on 20 Apr 1894 in Monroe County, Illinois.

iv. GEORGE SMISER was born on 17 May 1809 in Harrison County, Kentucky. He died on 22 Oct 1875 in Baton Rouge, Louisiana.

v. CATHERINE SMISER was born on 11 Nov 1811 in Harrison County, Kentucky.

vi. DARIUS LAYTON SMISER was born on 04 Jul 1814 in Garrard County, Kentucky. He died in 1909 in Bates County, Missouri.

vii. WILLIAM A. SMISER was born on 22 Oct 1817 in Harrison County, Kentucky. He died in Dec 1894. He married Helena P. Lair on 18 Sep 1844 in Lincoln County, Kentucky.

18. viii. MARY SMISER was born in Oct 1820. She died in 1891. She married JAMES FRAZER. He was born in 1807. He died in 1866.

ix. CELIA SMISER was born on 24 Dec 1825 in Harrison County, Kentucky. She died on 23 Jan 1875.

8. **MARY MAGDALINE[3] SMISER** (Mathias[2] Smyser, George[1] Schmeiser) was born about 1771 in York County, Pennsylvania. She died about 1812 in Jefferson County, Kentucky. She married William Abraham Fry, son of John Frye and Margaret (unknown) on 28 Sep 1794 in Hagerstown, Maryland. He was born about 1770. He died on 13 Sep 1821 in Jefferson County, Kentucky.

William Abraham Fry and Mary Magdaline Smiser had the following children:

i. GEORGE[4] FRY was born in 1796 in Kentucky. He died in 1821.

ii. SARAH FRY was born on 17 Aug 1799 in Jefferson County, Kentucky. She died on 25 Aug 1838.

iii. JOHN FRY was born on 11 Sep 1801 in Jefferson County, Kentucky. He died on 28 May 1885.

iv. NANCY ANN FRY was born on 29 Mar 1804 in Jefferson County, Kentucky. She died on 10 Sep 1888 in Jeffersonville, Indiana. She married George Swartz on 21 Aug 1823 in Clark County, Indiana. He was born on 18 Jan 1808 in Clark County, Indiana.

Notes for Nancy Ann Fry:
Seymour Daily Democrat newspaper, Seymour, IN
Tuesday 11 September 1888; Page 3, Column 5

THE TOMB

SWARTZ - At her home in Jeffersonville, Monday evening, September 10th, 1888, Mrs. Nancy Swartz, aged eighty-five years.

Mrs. Nancy Swartz, was the wife of Rev. George Swartz. Her maiden name was Fry and she was born near Middletown, KY, and was married to her husband in Clark County, IN, August 21, 1823, by Rev. Rezin Hammond.

To the couple were born twelve children, of whom the following survive: Wiley Swartz, Mrs. Lizzie Cook, Frank Swartz, Mrs. William Adams and Mrs. Laura Hollis.

Rev. and Mrs. Swartz were conceded to be the oldest living married couple in the state of Indiana, the husband being the oldest native born citizen, and the oldest Methodist minister. He was born in Clark County, Indiana, January 18, 1808, and, despite his old age, is a hale man.

    v.   JACOB FRY was born in 1806 in Jefferson County, Kentucky. He died about 1822.

    vi.   WILLIAM FRY was born in 1807 in Jefferson County, Kentucky. He died about 1822.

    vii.   ABRAHAM FRY was born in 1808 in Jefferson County, Kentucky. He died in 1838 in Jefferson County, Kentucky.

9.   MICHAEL[3] SMISER (Mathias[2] Smyser, George[1] Schmeiser) was born on 09 Feb 1772 in York County, Pennsylvania. He died on 08 Apr 1855 in Centerfield, Kentucky. He married (1) SALLY OGLESBY on 17 Sep 1797 in Jefferson County, Kentucky. He married (2) ELIZABETH ELLIS on 18 Dec 1804 in Shelby County, Kentucky.

Michael Smiser and Elizabeth Ellis had the following child:

    i.   MICHAEL[4] SMISER was born about 1810.

Generation 4

10.   SARAH[4] SMISER (John[3], Mathias[2] Smyser, George[1] Schmeiser) was born in 1804. She married JOHN BEIDLER GROVES. He was born on 13 Sep 1797 in Hawkins, Tennessee. He died in Sep 1853 in New Orleans, Louisiana.

More About John Beidler Groves:
Burial: 01 Sep 1853 in St. Louis No. 2 Cemetery, New Orleans, Louisiana.
Cause Of Death: Yellow Fever

John Beidler Groves and Sarah Smiser had the following children:

    i.   FANNY[5] GROVES was born on 04 Jul 1821 in Tennessee. She died on 22 Aug 1853 in New Orleans, Louisiana.

        More About Fanny Groves:
        Burial: 23 Aug 1853 in St. Louis No. 2 Cemetery, New Orleans, Louisiana Cause Of Death: Yellow Fever

    ii.   JACOB ROSCOE GROVES was born in 1826. He married Susan B. Roach in 1856.

    iii.   SARAH ELIZA GROVES was born on 09 May 1830. She died on 12 Aug 1853 in New Orleans, Louisiana.

More About Sarah Eliza Groves:
Burial: 13 Aug 1853 in St. Louis No. 2 Cemetery, New Orleans, Louisiana
Cause Of Death: Yellow Fever

iv.   MARY TURNEY GROVES was born on 06 Sep 1832 in New Orleans, Louisiana. She died on 27 Aug 1853.

More About Mary Turney Groves:
Burial: 28 Aug 1853 in St. Louis No. 2 Cemetery, New Orleans, Louisiana Cause Of Death: Yellow Fever

v.   JOHN SMISER GROVES was born in 1835 in Tennessee.

More About John Smiser Groves:
Military Service: Company D, 9th Tennessee Cavalry, C.S.A.

Notes for John Smiser Groves:
Served as Captain of Company D, 9th Kentucky Cavalry, C.S.A. Paroled at Gainesville, Alabama on May 11, 1865.
----

vi.   ELLEN SMISER GROVES was born on 19 Feb 1837. She died on 17 Aug 1853.

More About Ellen Smiser Groves:
Burial: Smiser-Booker Cemetery, Columbia, Tennessee

11.   **NANCY W.**[4] **SMISER** (John[3], Mathias[2] Smyser, George[1] Schmeiser) was born about 1805 in Maury County, Tennessee. She died before 1840. She married Edward Garland, son of Peter Garland and Mary Reamey on 14 May 1821 in Columbia, Tennessee. He was born before 1807 in Henry County, Virginia. He died before 05 Dec 1850.

Notes for Nancy W. Smiser:
Selina, Eliza and Mary were raised by their grandparents, John Smiser and Eve Mary Turney Smiser after about 1830.

Edward Garland and Nancy W. Smiser had the following children:

19.   i. SALINA J.[5] GARLAND was born in Feb 1823 in Tennessee. She died in Dec 1903 in Denver, Colorado. She married Claudius Buchanan Hall, son of Thomas James Hall and Emma Wallace on 20 Nov 1845 in Maury County, Tennessee. He was born on 21 Jan 1820 in Tennessee. He died between 05 Sep 1870-07 Jun 1880.

20.   ii. EDWARD WARREN GARLAND was born on 28 Oct 1825 in Giles County, Tennessee. He died on 12 May 1897 in Texas. He married (1) JULIA REBECCA KIMBELL, daughter of John M. Kimbell and Sarah Angelina Elliott before 1878. She was born on 31 Mar 1845 in Republic of Texas. She died on 26 Jan 1908 in Texas. He married (2) MARY EMELINE JENKINS, daughter of James Wilson Jenkins and Sarah Dowd on 18 Jun 1845 in Tishomingo County, Mississippi. She was born on 25 Oct 1827 in Chatham County, North Carolina. She died on 21 Feb 1887 in Hardin County, Tennessee.

    iii.   ELLEN GARLAND was born about 1829 in Tennessee.

           More About Ellen Garland:
           Living In: 1850 Living in the household of Mary Booker in Maury County, Tennessee.

    iv.   MARY GARLAND.

    v.   ELIZA GARLAND.

12.   ELIZA B.[4] SMISER (John[3], Mathias[2] Smyser, George[1] Schmeiser) was born about 1809 in Mississippi. She died in 1872. She married Spivey McKissack, son of Thomas McKissack and Lucy Edwards on 31 Oct 1842 in Maury County, Tennessee. He was born on 18 Sep 1790 in North Carolina. He died in 1864 in Columbia, Tennessee.

Spivey McKissack and Eliza B. Smiser had the following children:

    i.   MARY S.[5] MCKISSACK was born about 1844.

22.   ii. LUCY ANN MCKISSACK was born on 08 Nov 1846 in Spring Hill, Tennessee. She died in 1923 in Maury County, Tennessee. She married Thomas Gibson, son of Robert Gibson and Jane Adams on 01 Feb 1868 in Woodlawn, Tennessee. He was born on 20 Sep 1836 in Nashville, Tennessee. He died on 23 Nov 1917.

13.   ALFRED[4] SMISER (John[3], Mathias[2] Smyser, George[1] Schmeiser) was born about 1811 in Mississippi. He died in May 1865 in Helena, Arkansas. He married Catharine Crockett, daughter of George Crockett and Margaret Adams on 29 Jun 1852 in Davidson, Tennessee. She was born about 1827 in Tennessee.

More About Alfred Smiser:
Occupation: 1850; Farmer in Maury County, Tennessee
Occupation: 1860; Farmer, Planters Township, Phillips County, Arkansas

Alfred Smiser and Catharine Crockett had the following children:

    i.   WILLIAM[5] SMISER was born about 1854 in Tennessee.

    ii.   JOHN SMISER.

           Notes   for   John
           Smiser: Died young.

22.   iii. MARGARET ADAMS SMISER was born in 1865. She died in 1943. She married Harlan Bingham Miller on 19 Jun 1887. He was born on 29 Aug 1865. He died on 17 Sep 1909.

14.   ELLEN MATHENA[4] SMISER (John[3], Mathias[2] Smyser, George[1] Schmeiser) was born about 1814. She died in 1892. She married James Gray Booker, son of Peter R. Booker and Susannah Gray on 24 Feb 1835 in Maury County, Tennessee. He was born on 04 Nov 1809 in Williamson County, Tennessee. He died on 19 Aug 1846 in Maury County, Tennessee.

Notes for Ellen Mathena Smiser:
Inherited "Fairmont" from her parents.

More About James Gray Booker:
Burial: Smiser-Booker Cemetery, Columbia, Tennessee

James Gray Booker and Ellen Mathena Smiser had the following children:

    i.   SUSAN GRAY[5] BOOKER was born in 1835. She died in 1864.

23.   ii. MARY TURNEY BOOKER was born on 08 Nov 1837 in Columbia, Tennessee. She died on 22 Aug 1920. She married Britton Drake Clopton on 25 Nov 1858. He was born on 09 Mar 1835. He died on 04 Feb 1881 in Columbia, Maury County, Tennessee.

    iii.   SARA ELLEN BOOKER was born on 09 Nov 1839. She died on 29 Sep 1840.

        More About Sara Ellen Booker:
        Burial: Smiser-Booker Cemetery, Columbia, Tennessee

    iv.   JAMES GRAY BOOKER was born in 1841. He died in 1868.

    v.   ELLEN SMISER BOOKER was born in 1843. She died on 20 May 1869. She married Hoggatt Clopton on 10 Dec 1867. He was born on 06 Feb 1831 in Davidson, Tennessee. He died in 1912.

    vi.   JOHN LUCIEN BOOKER was born on 06 Oct 1846. He died on 17 Nov 1848.

        More About John Lucien Booker:
        Burial: Smiser-Booker Cemetery, Columbia, Tennessee

15.   **JAMES[4] SMISER** (John[3], Mathias[2] Smyser, George[1] Schmeiser) was born about 1820 in Maury County, Tennessee. He married Charlotte P. Booker on 27 Oct 1847 in Maury County, Tennessee. She was born about 1828 in Virginia.

More About James Smiser:
Occupation: 1850; Farmer in Maury County, Tennessee
Occupation: 1860; Farmer, Planters Township, Phillips County, Arkansas
Occupation: 1880; Druggist in Culleoka, Tennessee

James Smiser and Charlotte P. Booker had the following children:

24.   i. MERRITT BOOKER[5] SMISER was born on 22 Jul 1848 in Maury County, Tennessee. He died on 20 Jan 1929 in Culleoka, Tennessee. He married Lizzie Sparks Wilkes in 1879 in Maury County, Tennessee. She was born on 16 Oct 1853. She died in 1926.

    ii.   MARY E. SMISER was born about 1853 in Maury County, Tennessee.

    iii.   JOHN SMISER was born about 1859 in Arkansas.

    iv.   ALFRED SMISER was born about 1862 in Tennessee.

    v.   SALLY T. SMISER was born about 1868 in Tennessee.

16. **JOSEPH WARREN[4] SMISER** (John[3], Mathias[2] Smyser, George[1] Schmeiser) was born about 1822 in Tennessee. He died in 1884. He married Martha Page Frierson, daughter of John William Frierson and Lucy Ann Mosby on 23 Dec 1856 in Tennessee. She was born about 1838 in Tennessee.

More About Joseph Warren Smiser:
Occupation: 1850; Lawyer in Maury County, Tennessee
Occupation: 1860; Farmer, Planters Township, Arkansas
Military Service: Company H, 1st Arkansas Cavalry, C.S.A.

Notes for Joseph Warren Smiser:
Captured April 10, 1864 in Phillips County, Arkansas and sent to Camp Chase in Columbus, Ohio, arriving on May 17, 1864. Transferred to Point Lookout, Maryland on February 12, 1865. Released at Camp Lee, Virginia on May 30, 1865.

Joseph Warren Smiser and Martha Page Frierson had the following child:

25.   i. LUCY PAGE[5] SMISER was born in 1859 in Arkansas. She married Joseph Alexander Titcomb on 10 Aug 1881. He was born on 10 Aug 1856 in Columbia, Maury County, Tennessee.

17. **MARIA[4] SMISER** (John[3], Mathias[2] Smyser, George[1] Schmeiser) was born in 1824. She died on 10 Feb 1849. She married **CHARLES L. NELSON**.

More About Maria Smiser:
Burial: Smiser-Booker Cemetery, Columbia, Tennessee

Charles L. Nelson and Maria Smiser had the following child:

     i. JOHN MATTHEW[5] NELSON was born on 30 Dec 1848. He died on 20 Oct 1849.

18. **MARY[4] SMISER** (George[3], Mathias[2] Smyser, George[1] Schmeiser) was born in Oct 1820. She died in 1891. She married **JAMES FRAZER**. He was born in 1807. He died in 1866.

James Frazer and Mary Smiser had the following child:

26.   i. NOAH[5] FRAZER was born in 1841. He died in 1897. He married **MARY KATHERINE DUNLAP**.

Generation 5

19. **SALINA J.[5] GARLAND** (Nancy W.[4] Smiser, John[3] Smiser, Mathias[2] Smyser, George[1] Schmeiser) was born in Feb 1823 in Tennessee. She died in Dec 1903 in Denver, Colorado. She married Claudius Buchanan Hall, son of Thomas James Hall and Emma Wallace on 20 Nov 1845 in Maury County, Tennessee. He was born on 21 Jan 1820 in Tennessee. He died between 05 Sep 1870-07 Jun 1880.

More About Salina J. Garland:
Burial: 27 Dec 1903 in Fairmount Cemetery, Denver, Colorado
Living In: 1880 Lafayette, Christian County, Kentucky
Living In: Bet. 1885-1894 Nashville, Tennessee
Living In: 1900 Denver, Colorado

More About Claudius Buchanan Hall:
Living In: 1870 in Lafayette, Kentucky
Occupation: 1850 in Christian County, Kentucky; Physician

Occupation: 1860 in Christian County, Kentucky; Physician
Occupation: 1870 in Lafayette, Christian County, Kentucky; Physician

Claudius Buchanan Hall and Salina J. Garland had the following children:

  i. MARY ELLEN[6] HALL was born in Sep 1849 in Kentucky.

  ii. LIZZIE C. HALL was born in Nov 1859 in Kentucky.

    More About Lizzie C. Hall:
    Living In: 1880 Living with her mother in Lafayette, Christian County, Kentucky.
    Living In: 1900   Living with her mother in Denver, Colorado.

27. iii. ALLEN GARLAND HALL was born on 12 Jul 1862 in Kentucky. He died on 28 Nov 1915 in
    Nashville, Tennessee. He married Lillie Carter Gunn, daughter of Wesley Gunn and
    Martha Addie Grinter on 26 Feb 1885 in Kentucky. She was born on 02 Nov 1864 in
    Kentucky. She died on 08 Aug 1958 in Cadiz, Kentucky.

  iv. CHARLIE HALL was born about 1865 in Kentucky.

20. **EDWARD WARREN[5] GARLAND** (Nancy W.[4] Smiser, John[3] Smiser, Mathias[2] Smyser, George[1]
Schmeiser) was born on 28 Oct 1825 in Giles County, Tennessee. He died on 12 May 1897 in
Texas. He married (1) **JULIA REBECCA KIMBELL**, daughter of John M. Kimbell and Sarah Angelina
Elliott before 1878. She was born on 31 Mar 1845 in Republic of Texas. She died on 26 Jan
1908 in Texas. He married (2) **MARY EMELINE JENKINS**, daughter of James Wilson Jenkins and
Sarah Dowd on 18 Jun 1845 in Tishomingo County, Mississippi. She was born on 25 Oct 1827
in Chatham County, North Carolina. She died on 21 Feb 1887 in Hardin County, Tennessee.

More About Edward Warren Garland:
Burial: Garland Cemetery, Red River County, Texas
Living In: 1845 With his uncle, Peter Garland, in Tishomingo County, Mississippi, two doors
away from the home of Mary Emeline Jenkins
Living In: Feb 1868 Red River County, Texas
Occupation: 1850 in Tishomingo County, Mississippi; Merchant
Occupation: 1880 in Precinct 7, Red River County, Texas; Farmer
Military Service: Bet. 13 Sep 1847-10 Jul 1848 in Mexican War; Company C, Second
Mississippi Infantry, U.S. Army
Military Service: Civil War for C.S.A.
Property: 1869 in Bowie County, Texas; 300 Acres
Property: 1870 in Bowie County, Texas; 300 Acres
Property:1880 in Red River County, Texas; 36 Acres Improved and 50 Acres
Unimproved
Property: 1888 in Bowie County, Texas; 108 Acres and 8 city lots in DeKalb
Property: 1889 in Bowie County, Texas; 108 Acres and 8 city lots in DeKalb
Property: 1896 in Bowie County, Texas; 110 Acres and 7 city lots in DeKalb
Property: 1897 in Bowie County, Texas; 110 Acres and 7 city lots in DeKalb

Notes for Edward Warren Garland:
Mustered in for Mexican War at Farmington, Mississippi. Mustered out in Vicksburg, Mississippi.

November 25, 1869 Red River County, Texas voter registration shows Edward having lived in
Red River County and Texas 22 months at that time.

More About Julia Rebecca Kimbell:

Burial: Garland Cemetery, Red River County, Texas
Cause Of Death: Infection from a rat bite to her hand while reaching into a corn bin in her barn
Living In: 1900 With her Garland children in Commisioner Precinct 3, Bowie County, Texas
Occupation: 1860 in DeKalb, Texas; Seamstress
Property: 1886 in Bowie County, Texas; 18 Acres

Edward Warren Garland and Julia Rebecca Kimbell had the following children:

28.   i. JOSEPH EDWARD[6] GARLAND was born on 17 Mar 1878 in Red River County, Texas. He died on 01 Sep 1946 in Lamesa, Dawson County, Texas. He married Lou Ethel Bynum, daughter of Alfred Baker Bynum and Dorinda Sandal Baird on 21 May 1908 in Brownfield, Texas. She was born on 25 Apr 1890 in Whitewright, Grayson County, Texas. She died on 17 Sep 1969 in Lamesa, Dawson County, Texas.

29.   ii. EMMA GEORGIE IRENE GARLAND was born on 23 Mar 1880 in Annona, Texas. She died on 17 Dec 1969 in Kerrville, Texas. She married LeRoy Ardis Edwards in May 1921 in Roscoe, Texas. He was born on 27 Feb 1881 in Sulphur Springs, Texas. He died on 05 Dec 1951 in Loraine, Texas.

     iii. RUFUS SMIZER MCKINNEY GARLAND was born on 03 Sep 1882 in Texas. He died on 07 Feb 1919 in North Atlantic Ocean (Returning from France after World War One).

More About Rufus Smizer McKinney Garland:
Burial: Loraine, Texas
Cause Of Death: Spanish Flu
Occupation: 1910 in Roscoe, Texas; Drug Store Prescriptionist
Occupation: 1917 in Loraine, Texas; Pharmacist
Military Service: 1918 in France; World War One (Medic)
Military Service: Spanish American War

Notes for Rufus Smizer McKinney Garland:
Died at sea on the way home from World War One military service in France due to the Great Flu Epidemic.
Never Married.

30.   iv. MAGGIE AUGUSTA ESTELLE GARLAND was born in Aug 1884 in DeKalb, Texas. She died on 29 Jan 1955 in Sweetwater, Texas. She married Barna Haney, son of William Daniel Haney and Mamie H. Harkins on 24 May 1911 in Roscoe, Texas. He was born on 30 Nov 1887 in Temple, Bell County, Texas. He died on 27 Jan 1957 in Roscoe, Texas.

More About Mary Emeline Jenkins:
Burial: Roberts Cemetery, Conce, Hardin County, Tennessee
Cause Of Death: Consumption

More About Edward Warren Garland and Mary Emeline Jenkins:
Marriage Fact: 16 Jun 1845 in Date of Marriage Bond
Marriage Fact: Ceremony performed by J. C. Lowery, J.P.
Marriage Fact: Garland Family Oral History; Marriage lasted only one day.
Marriage Fact: Surety: G. L. Goff

21.   LUCY ANN[5] MCKISSACK (Eliza B.[4] Smiser, John[3] Smiser, Mathias[2] Smyser, George[1] Schmeiser) was born on 08 Nov 1846 in Spring Hill, Tennessee. She died in 1923 in Maury County, Tennessee. She married Thomas Gibson, son of Robert Gibson and Jane Adams on 01 Feb 1868

in Woodlawn, Tennessee. He was born on 20 Sep 1836 in Nashville, Tennessee. He died on 23 Nov 1917.

Thomas Gibson and Lucy Ann McKissack had the following children:

    i.   JANE ADAMS[6] GIBSON.

    ii.   ELIZA GIBSON was born on 12 Apr 1872. She died on 27 Oct 1956 in Maury County, Tennessee.

22.   **MARGARET ADAMS[5] SMISER** (Alfred[4], John[3], Mathias[2] Smyser, George[1] Schmeiser) was born in 1865. She died in 1943. She married Harlan Bingham Miller on 19 Jun 1887. He was born on 29 Aug 1865. He died on 17 Sep 1909.

Harlan Bingham Miller and Margaret Adams Smiser had the following children:

31.   i. WILLIAM ALFRED[6] MILLER was born on 13 Sep 1890. He died on 31 May 1969. He married Sara Virginia Swindell on 20 Jun 1923. She was born on 27 Oct 1899. She died on 11 May 1987.

32.   ii. KATHERINE BINGHAM MILLER was born in 1896. She married FRANK R. MCLEAN. He was born in 1896.

    iii.   MARGARET MILLER.

    iv.   GEORGE MILLER.

23.   **MARY TURNEY[5] BOOKER** (Ellen Mathena[4] Smiser, John[3] Smiser, Mathias[2] Smyser, George[1] Schmeiser) was born on 08 Nov 1837 in Columbia, Tennessee. She died on 22 Aug 1920. She married Britton Drake Clopton on 25 Nov 1858. He was born on 09 Mar 1835. He died on 04 Feb 1881 in Columbia, Maury County, Tennessee.

Britton Drake Clopton and Mary Turney Booker had the following children:

    i.   JAMES BOOKER[6] CLOPTON was born on 28 Jan 1860. He died on 06 Aug 1883.

    ii.   BRITTON DRAKE CLOPTON was born on 28 Feb 1862. He died on 04 Sep 1862.

    iii.   CARRIE HOGGATT CLOPTON was born on 19 Nov 1863 in Tennessee. She died on 18 Jul 1939 in Columbia, Maury County, Tennessee. She married DAVID SINCLAIR GLASS.

    iv.   SUSAN CLOPTON was born on 15 Jan 1866. She married Samuel Holding on 07 Dec 1898.

    v.   ELLEN SMISER CLOPTON was born on 06 Dec 1868 in Nashville, Tennessee. She married Robert S. McCarty on 21 Sep 1897. He was born in Helena, Arkansas.

    vi.   BRITTON DRAKE CLOPTON was born on 09 Apr 1871. He died on 06 Nov 1924 in Bowling Green, Kentucky. He married ELIZABETH ISAACS.

    vii.   JOHN ANDERSON CLOPTON.

24.   **MERRITT BOOKER[5] SMISER** (James[4], John[3], Mathias[2] Smyser, George[1] Schmeiser) was born on 22 Jul 1848 in Maury County, Tennessee. He died on 20 Jan 1929 in Culleoka, Tennessee. He married Lizzie Sparks Wilkes in 1879 in Maury County, Tennessee. She was born on 16 Oct 1853. She died in 1926.

Merritt Booker Smiser and Lizzie Sparks Wilkes had the following children:

    i.   WALLACE[6] SMISER was born in Dec 1881.

    ii.   BOOKER SMISER was born in Nov 1883.

    iii.   ROBERT W. SMISER was born in 1884 in Tennessee.

33.   iv. CHARLOTTE ELVIRA SMISER was born in Oct 1885 in Culleoka, Tennessee. She died on 15 Nov 1971 in Winter Garden, Florida. She married BERT HANSE ROPER. He was born on 30 Jan 1879 in Winter Garden, Florida. He died on 28 Jul 1941 in Winter Garden, Florida.

    v.   MERRITT B. SMISER was born in 1885 in Tennessee.

25.   LUCY PAGE[5] SMISER (Joseph Warren[4], John[3], Mathias[2] Smyser, George[1] Schmeiser) was born in 1859 in Arkansas. She married Joseph Alexander Titcomb on 10 Aug 1881. He was born on 10 Aug 1856 in Columbia, Maury County, Tennessee.

Joseph Alexander Titcomb and Lucy Page Smiser had the following children:

    i.   HIRAM B.[6] TITCOMB was born about 1884 in Columbia, Maury County, Tennessee.

    ii.   WARREN SMISER TITCOMB was born on 12 Mar 1890.

26.   NOAH[5] FRAZER (Mary[4] Smiser, George[3] Smiser, Mathias[2] Smyser, George[1] Schmeiser) was born in 1841. He died in 1897. He married MARY KATHERINE DUNLAP.

Noah Frazer and Mary Katherine Dunlap had the following children:

    i.   WILLIAM[6] FRAZER.

    ii.   EUGENIA FRAZER.

    iii.   MARY K. FRAZER.

Generation 6

27.   ALLEN GARLAND[6] HALL (Salina J.[5] Garland, Nancy W.[4] Smiser, John[3] Smiser, Mathias[2] Smyser, George[1] Schmeiser) was born on 12 Jul 1862 in Kentucky. He died on 28 Nov 1915 in Nashville, Tennessee. He married Lillie Carter Gunn, daughter of Wesley Gunn and Martha Addie Grinter on 26 Feb 1885 in Kentucky. She was born on 02 Nov 1864 in Kentucky. She died on 08 Aug 1958 in Cadiz, Kentucky.

More About Allen Garland Hall:
Burial: Mount Olivet Cemetery, Nashville, Tennessee
Occupation: 1900 in Nashville, Tennessee; High School Teacher
Occupation: 1910 in Nashville, Tennessee; University Professor
Occupation: Dean of Vanderbilt University School of Law

Notes for Allen Garland Hall:
Dean of Law, Vanderbilt University.

More About Lillie Carter Gunn:
Burial: Mount Olivet Cemetery, Nashville, Tennessee

More About Allen Garland Hall and Lillie Carter Gunn:
Marriage Fact: Ceremony performed by Reverend V. Elgin

Allen Garland Hall and Lillie Carter Gunn had the following children:

  i.   GLENN ANDREWS[7] HALL was born on 24 Nov 1885 in Tennessee. He died on 23 May 1953 in Tennessee.

       More About Glenn Andrews Hall:
       Living In: 1910 Living with his parents in Nashville, Tennessee.
       Occupation: 1910 in Nashville, Tennessee; Newspaper Editor
       Military Service: U. S. Marine Corps, World War One

34. ii. FITZGERALD HALL was born on 06 Dec 1889 in Nashville, Tennessee. He died on 07 Feb 1946 in Nashville, Tennessee. He married ELIZABETH MURPHY GARDNER.

28. **JOSEPH EDWARD[6] GARLAND** (Edward Warren[5], Nancy W.[4] Smiser, John[3] Smiser, Mathias[2] Smyser, George[1] Schmeiser) was born on 17 Mar 1878 in Red River County, Texas. He died on 01 Sep 1946 in Lamesa, Dawson County, Texas. He married Lou Ethel Bynum, daughter of Alfred Baker Bynum and Dorinda Sandal Baird on 21 May 1908 in Brownfield, Texas. She was born on 25 Apr 1890 in Whitewright, Grayson County, Texas. She died on 17 Sep 1969 in Lamesa, Dawson County, Texas.

More About Joseph Edward Garland:
Burial: 03 Sep 1946 in Lamesa Cemetery, Lamesa, Texas
Cause Of Death: Cerebral Hemorrhage
Living In: 1900 With his mother and siblings in Bowie County, Texas
Occupation: 1900 in Commisioner Precinct 3, Bowie County, Texas; Day Laborer
Occupation: 1910 in Dawson County, Texas; Lawyer
Occupation: 1918 in Lamesa, Texas; County Judge and Attorney
Occupation: 1920 in Lamesa, Texas; Attorney at Law
Occupation: 1930 in Lamesa, Texas; Independant Lawyer
Occupation: 1940 in Lamesa, Texas; Attorney at Law
Military Service: Spanish American War

More About Lou Ethel Bynum:
Burial: 19 Sep 1969 in Lamesa Cemetery, Lamesa, Texas Cause Of Death: Heart Disease

Joseph Edward Garland and Lou Ethel Bynum had the following children:

  i.   EDWARD BYNUM[7] GARLAND was born on 15 Jun 1909 in Texas. He died on 30 Oct 1986 in Seminole, Texas.

       More About Edward Bynum Garland:
       Burial: Lamesa Cemetery, Lamesa, Texas
       Living In: 1930 Living with his parents in Lamesa, Texas
       Living In: 1940 Living with his parents in Lamesa, Texas
       Occupation: 1940 in Lamesa, Dawson County, Texas; Stock Farmer Military
       Service: Bet. 05 Sep 1942-15 Nov 1945 ; U.S. Army, World War Two

36. ii. MARGARET DORINDA GARLAND was born on 01 Oct 1911 in Lamesa, Dawson County, Texas. She died on 29 Apr 2005 in Lubbock, Texas. She married James Mack Noble, son of James Mack Noble and Rosia Lee Carter on 01 Jan 1933 in

Lamesa, Texas. He was born on 29 Jun 1898 in Texas. He died on 07 Sep 1961 in O'Donnell, Texas.

36.　　　iii. JAMES GARLAND was born on 20 Sep 1918 in Lamesa, Dawson County, Texas. He died on 25 Feb 1988 in Hobbs, New Mexico. He married (1) EVA MAE WATERS on 01 Jun 1950 in Dawson County, Texas. She was born about 1924. He married DOROTHY (UNKNOWN).

29.　**EMMA GEORGIE IRENE**[6] **GARLAND** (Edward Warren[5], Nancy W.[4] Smiser, John[3] Smiser, Mathias[2] Smyser, George[1] Schmeiser) was born on 23 Mar 1880 in Annona, Texas. She died on 17 Dec 1969 in Kerrville, Texas. She married LeRoy Ardis Edwards in May 1921 in Roscoe, Texas. He was born on 27 Feb 1881 in Sulphur Springs, Texas. He died on 05 Dec 1951 in Loraine, Texas.

More About Emma Georgie Irene Garland:
Burial: 20 Dec 1969 in Loraine Cemetery,Loraine, Texas
Cause Of Death: Broncho Pneumonia and Arteriosclerosis
Living In: 1920 Lamesa, Texas with sister Estelle and family.
Occupation: 1920 in Lamesa, Texas; Teacher

More About LeRoy Ardis Edwards:
Burial: 07 Dec 1951 in Loraine Cemetery, Loraine, Texas
Cause Of Death: Carcinoma of Lung
Occupation: 1930 in Loraine, Texas; Lumber Yard Manager
Occupation: 1940 in Olton, Texas; Retail Lumber Yard Manager

Notes for LeRoy Ardis Edwards:
Discovered and owned, with his brother Walter, "Baking Powder" gold mine in New Mexico.

LeRoy Ardis Edwards and Emma Georgie Irene Garland had the following child:
37.　　　i. ROY GARLAND[7] EDWARDS was born on 30 May 1922 in Loraine, Texas. He died on 14 Oct 1974 in Tampa, Florida. He married Maribel Savage on 08 Apr 1944 in Lubbock, Texas. She was born on 22 Jun 1926 in Sherman, texas. She died on 14 Feb 2010 in Tampa, Florida.

30.　**MAGGIE AUGUSTA ESTELLE**[6] **GARLAND** (Edward Warren[5], Nancy W.[4] Smiser, John[3] Smiser, Mathias[2] Smyser, George[1] Schmeiser) born in Aug 1884 in DeKalb, Texas. She died on 29 Jan 1955 in Sweetwater, Texas. She married Barna Haney, son of William Daniel Haney and Mamie H. Harkins on 24 May 1911 in Roscoe, Texas. He was born on 30 Nov 1887 in Temple, Bell County, Texas. He died on 27 Jan 1957 in Roscoe, Texas.

More About Maggie Augusta Estelle Garland:
Burial: 31 Jan 1955 in Roscoe Cemetery, Roscoe, Texas Cause Of Death: Cerebral Hemorhage
Living In: 1910 Living with her brother, Rufus Garland, in Roscoe, Texas
Living In: 1920 Lamesa, Texas
Living In:1930 Roscoe, Texas
Living In: 1955 Roscoe, Texas
Occupation: 1910 in Roscoe, Texas; Dry Goods Saleslady

More About Barna Haney:
Burial: 28 Jan 1957 in Roscoe Cemetery, Roscoe, Texas
Living In: 1900 Bell County, Texas
Living In: 1910 Living with his parents in Roscoe, Texas

Occupation: 1910 in Roscoe, Texas; Furniture Sales Clerk
Occupation: 1920 in Lamesa, Texas; Clerk in Meyers Drug Company
Occupation: 1930 in Roscoe, Texas; Druggist in Drug Store
Occupation: 1932 in Roscoe, Texas; President of Board of Education
Occupation: 1940 in Roscoe, Texas; Pharmacist and Drug Store owner, Roscoe, Texas

Notes for Barna Haney:
Owned Haney Drug Store, Roscoe, Texas. Mayor and School Board Member of Roscoe, Texas.

More About Barna Haney and Maggie Augusta Estelle Garland:
Marriage License: 23 May 1911 in Nolan County, Texas
Marriage Fact: Married by Rev. J. W. Smith, M. E. Church South, Roscoe, Texas.

Barna Haney and Maggie Augusta Estelle Garland had the following children:

38.   i.   WILLIAM GARLAND[7] HANEY was born on 11 May 1912 in Roscoe, Texas. He died on 19
                 Jan 1988 in Lubbock, Texas. He married Allie Pearl Dunn, daughter of Yanks Dunn
                 and Ada Branson on 04 Oct 1942 in Roscoe, Texas. She was born on 07 Oct 1922 in
                 Burleson, Texas. She died on 29 Apr 2007 in Roscoe, Texas.

39.   ii.   MARY JULIA HANEY was born on 16 Aug 1916. She died on 25 Jun 1996 in
                 Clarkesville, Texas. She married Joseph Dellinger Garland, son of Wirt Robert
                 Garland and Lola Prudence Dellinger on 21 Jun 1942 in Roscoe, Texas. He was
                 born on 07 Dec 1914 in Annona, Texas. He died on 16 Aug 1973 in Clarkesville,
                 Texas.

31.   **WILLIAM ALFRED**[6] **MILLER** (Margaret Adams[5] Smiser, Alfred[4] Smiser, John[3] Smiser, Mathias[2]
      Smyser, George[1] Schmeiser) was born on 13 Sep 1890. He died on 31 May 1969. He married Sara
      Virginia Swindell on 20 Jun 1923. She was born on 27 Oct 1899. She died on 11 May 1987.

      William Alfred Miller and Sara Virginia Swindell had the following children:

             i.   WILLIAM ALFRED[7] MILLER was born in Sep 1929. He died on 25 Feb 1931.

            ii.   SUSAN DOUGLAS MILLER was born on 08 Dec 1931. She married Hartwell
                  Dee Hooper on 20 Jun 1953.

           iii.   DAVID HOLLINGSWORTH MILLER was born on 13 Jul 1933. He died on 14 Jul 1933.

            iv.   JOHN AVERY MILLER was born on 14 Apr 1936. He died on 14 Apr 1936.

             v.   HARLAN BINGHAM MILLER was born on 15 Jul 1937. He died on 20 Jun 1959.
                  He married DOROTHY CARLTON WILKINS.

            vi.   RICHARD CROCKETT MILLER was born on 18 Jul 1940.

32.   **KATHERINE BINGHAM**[6] **MILLER** (Margaret Adams[5] Smiser, Alfred[4] Smiser, John[3] Smiser,
      Mathias[2] Smyser, George[1] Schmeiser) was born in 1896. She married **FRANK R. MCLEAN**. He
      was born in 1896.

      Frank R. McLean and Katherine Bingham Miller had the following children:

             i.   KATHERINE[7] MCLEAN was born in 1920. She married GERALD TAYLOR.

            ii.   MARGARET MCLEAN was born in 1923. She married SONNY KREHER.

iii.   GEORGE MCLEAN was born in 1925. He married MARTHA (UNKNOWN).

iv.   ANNE MCLEAN was born in 1928. She married LARRY NOBLE. She married JAMES CRAWFORD HENDERSON.

33.   CHARLOTTE ELVIRA^6 SMISER (Merritt Booker^5, James^4, John^3, Mathias^2 Smyser, George^1 Schmeiser) was born in Oct 1885 in Culleoka, Tennessee. She died on 15 Nov 1971 in Winter Garden, Florida. She married **BERT HANSE ROPER**. He was born on 30 Jan 1879 in Winter Garden, Florida. He died on 28 Jul 1941 in Winter Garden, Florida.

Bert Hanse Roper and Charlotte Elvira Smiser had the following children:

i.   FRANK BOOKER^7 ROPER was born in Williston, Florida. He married VIRGINIA L. BROOKS.

ii.   CHARLOTTE ELIZABETH ROPER.

Generation 7

34.   FITZGERALD^7 HALL (Allen Garland^6, Salina J.^{5} Garland, Nancy W.^{4} Smiser, John^3 Smiser, Mathias^2 Smyser, George^1 Schmeiser) was born on 06 Dec 1889 in Nashville, Tennessee. He died on 07 Feb 1946 in Nashville, Tennessee. He married **ELIZABETH MURPHY GARDNER**.

More About Fitzgerald Hall:
Occupation: President of Nashville, Chattanooga and St. Louis Railroad
Occupation: Assistant United States District Attorney
Occupation: Law Professor at Vanderbilt University School of Law

Notes for Fitzgerald Hall:
President of the Nashville, Chattanooga and Saint Louis Railroad.

Fitzgerald Hall and Elizabeth Murphy Gardner had the following children:

i.   ELIZABETH GARDNER^8 HALL. She married WILLIAM MOORE CLARK.

ii.   MARY FITZGERALD HALL. She married ALEX PIRTLE.

35.   MARGARET DORINDA^7 GARLAND (Joseph Edward^6, Edward Warren^5, Nancy W.^{4} Smiser, John^3 Smiser, Mathias^2 Smyser, George^1 Schmeiser) was born on 01 Oct 1911 in Lamesa, Dawson County, Texas. She died on 29 Apr 2005 in Lubbock, Texas. She married James Mack Noble, son of James Mack Noble and Rosia Lee Carter on 01 Jan 1933 in Lamesa, Texas. He was born on 29 Jun 1898 in Texas. He died on 07 Sep 1961 in O'Donnell, Texas.

More About Margaret Dorinda Garland:
Burial: 03 May 2005 in O'Donnell Cemetery, O'Donnell, Texas

Notes for Margaret Dorinda Garland:
    Lubbock Avalanche-Journal
Obituary of Margaret Garland Noble
Published: Monday, May 02, 2005

Margaret Garland Noble, 93, of Lubbock and formerly of ODonnell died Friday, April 29, 2005 at Grace House in Lubbock. She was born Sept. 30, 1911 in Lamesa. She married James Mack Noble, Jr. Jan. 1, 1933 in Lamesa. He preceded her in death in 1961.

Mrs. Noble was the daughter of Joseph Edward and Ethel Garland, who were early pioneer settlers in Dawson and Lynn counties. She was a world traveler, seeing places like China, Australia, New Zealand and Central America. In 1981, she and her family traveled to Scandanavia and Russia.

Margaret was employed by the U.S. Postal Service as a mail carrier. She belonged to Tuesday Bridge and Study Club in ODonnell.

Two brothers, James and Edward, also precede her in death.

Survivors include: two sons, Edward Garland of San Francisco Bay Area, Calif. and James Mack, III of Longview; two grandchildren; and two great-grandchildren.

Services will be 4 p.m. Tuesday at First United Methodist Church in ODonnell with the Rev. Kenneth Peterson officiating.

Burial will be in ODonnell Cemetery.

The family suggests memorial to the ODonnell Cemetery Association or a charity of choice.

Birth date is from birth certificate.

More About James Mack Noble:
Burial: 09 Sep 1961 in O'Donnell Cemetery, O'Donnell, Texas
Cause Of Death: Acute Coronary Thrombosis
Occupation: 1940 in O'Donnell, Texas; Post Master of U.S. Post Office
Occupation: 1961 in O'Donnell, Texas; Mail Carrier
Military Service: World War One

James Mack Noble and Margaret Dorinda Garland had the following children:

      i.   JAMES MACK[8] NOBLE was born on 10 Dec 1933 in Dawson County, Texas. He married JESSICA (UNKNOWN).

      ii.   EDWARD GARLAND NOBLE was born on 19 Aug 1936 in Dawson County, Texas.

36.   **JAMES[7] GARLAND** (Joseph Edward[6], Edward Warren[5], Nancy W.[4] Smiser, John[3] Smiser, Mathias[2] Smyser, George[1] Schmeiser) was born on 20 Sep 1918 in Lamesa, Dawson County, Texas. He died on 25 Feb 1988 in Hobbs, New Mexico. He married (1) **EVA MAE WATERS** on 01 Jun 1950 in Dawson County, Texas. She was born about 1924. He married **DOROTHY (UNKNOWN)**.

More About James Garland:
Burial: Dawson County Cemetery, Lamesa, Dawson County, Texas
Occupation: 1940 in Honolulu, Hawaii Territory; Medical Department, Tripler General Hospital, U.S. Army
Military Service: Bet. 1940-1945; World War Two

Notes for James Garland:
Present during Japanese attack on Pearl Harbor, December 7, 1941. Served in Europe- Normandy to V.E. Day.
Divorced from Eva Waters on January 16, 1974 in Gaines County, Texas.

James Garland and Eva Mae Waters had the following children:

      i.   MARGARET LOU[8] GARLAND. She married MIKE RYAN.

    ii.   JAMES GARLAND.

37.   **ROY GARLAND[7] EDWARDS** (Emma Georgie Irene[6] Garland, Edward Warren[5] Garland, Nancy W.[4] Smiser, John[3] Smiser, Mathias[2] Smyser, George[1] Schmeiser) was born on 30 May 1922 in Loraine, Texas. He died on 14 Oct 1974 in Tampa, Florida. He married Maribel Savage on 08 Apr 1944 in Lubbock, Texas. She was born on 22 Jun 1926 in Sherman, texas. She died on 14 Feb 2010 in Tampa, Florida.

More About Roy Garland Edwards:
Burial: Pleasant Grove Cemetery, Durant, Florida
Cause Of Death: Heart Failure
Military Service: Bet. 1942-1964; U.S. Air Force (Major)

More About Maribel Savage:
Burial: Pleasant Grove Cemetery, Durant, Florida Military Service: Bet. 1942-1964

Roy Garland Edwards and Maribel Savage had the following children:

    i.   DAVID GARLAND[8] EDWARDS was born on 21 May 1945 in Fort Sumner, New Mexico. He married Hope Ellen Stewart on 09 Mar 1968 in Tampa, Florida. She was born on 27 Jun 1949 in South Perry, Ohio.

    ii.   ROBERT MARION EDWARDS was born on 11 Dec 1946 in Lubbock, Texas. He died on 13 Feb 2010 in San Francisco, California.

38.   **WILLIAM GARLAND[7] HANEY** (Maggie Augusta Estelle[6] Garland, Edward Warren[5] Garland, Nancy W.[4] Smiser, John[3] Smiser, Mathias[2] Smyser, George[1] Schmeiser) was born on 11 May 1912 in Roscoe, Texas. He died on 19 Jan 1988 in Lubbock, Texas. He married Allie Pearl Dunn, daughter of Yanks Dunn and Ada Branson on 04 Oct 1942 in Roscoe, Texas. She was born on 07 Oct 1922 in Burleson, Texas. She died on 29 Apr 2007 in Roscoe, Texas.

More About William Garland Haney:
Burial: Roscoe Cemetery, Roscoe, Texas
Living In: 1940 Living with his parents in Roscoe, Texas
Occupation: 1940 in Roscoe, Texas; Retail Drug Clerk
Occupation: Pharmacist
Military Service: Enlisted at Lubbock, Texas, January 15, 1942 in U.S. Army for World War Two

Notes for William Garland Haney: Held rank of SSgt. while in U.S. Army.

More About Allie Pearl Dunn:
Burial: Roscoe Cemetery, Roscoe, Texas

Notes for Allie Pearl Dunn:
From THE SWEETWATER (TX) REPORTER

(4/30/2007): Allie Pearl Haney

Funeral services for Allie Pearl Haney, 84, of Roscoe will be held at 10 a.m. Tuesday, May 1, 2007, in the First United Methodist Church of Roscoe with Pastor Tony Wofford and the Rev. Vernon Baker officiating.

Burial will follow in the Roscoe Cemetery under the direction of McCoy Funeral Home of Roscoe.

The family will receive friends from 6-8 p.m. Monday, April 30, 2007, in the funeral home.

Mrs. Haney died Sunday, April 29, 2007, in Roscoe.

She was born on Oct. 7, 1922, in Burleson. She married William Garland Haney on Oct. 4, 1942, in Roscoe. Mrs. Haney was a member of the First United Methodist Church of Roscoe, where she taught Sunday school for many, many years. She lived most of her life in Roscoe, where she and her husband owned and operated Haney Drug and Haney Jewelry. She was a graduate of Roscoe High School. Mrs. Haney was a friend to all and is remembered by her family as their "One True Pearl."

Survivors include two daughters, Peggy Sue Parrot and her husband, Henry Don, of Roscoe, and Jackie Hackfeld and her husband, Keith, of Snyder; one son, Bill Haney and his wife, Nita, of Kansas City, Mo.; one sister, Peggy Richburg and her husband, Charles, of Roscoe; one brother, Buster Dunn and his wife, Wanda, of Roscoe; eight grandchildren and nine great-grandchildren.

She was preceded in death by her husband, William Haney, on Jan. 19, 1988.

William Garland Haney and Allie Pearl Dunn had the following children:

    i. WILLIAM GARLAND[8] HANEY JR. was born on 21 Jun 1944 in Randolph A.F.B., Texas. He married Nita Ann Buckner in Roscoe, Texas. She was born on 15 Jan 1945.

    ii. PEGGY SUSAN HANEY was born on 29 Jan 1950. She married Henry Don Parrott in Roscoe, Texas. He was born on 05 Nov 1943.

    iii. JACKIE ANN HANEY was born on 01 Feb 1958 in Sweetwater, Texas. She married Keith Alfred Hackfeld in Roscoe, Texas.

39. **MARY JULIA[7] HANEY** (Maggie Augusta Estelle[6] Garland, Edward Warren[5] Garland, Nancy W.[4] Smiser, John[3] Smiser, Mathias[2] Smyser, George[1] Schmeiser) was born on 16 Aug 1916. She died on 25 Jun 1996 in Clarkesville, Texas. She married Joseph Dellinger Garland, son of Wirt Robert Garland and Lola Prudence Dellinger on 21 Jun 1942 in Roscoe, Texas. He was born on 07 Dec 1914 in Annona, Texas. He died on 16 Aug 1973 in Clarkesville, Texas.

More About Mary Julia Haney:
Burial: 29 Jun 1996 in Garland Cemetery, Annona, Texas
Living In: 1940 Living with her parents in Roscoe, Texas.
Occupation: 1940 in Roscoe, Texas; Music Teacher
Occupation: Music Teacher, Pianist, Organist

More About Joseph Dellinger
Garland:
Burial: 18 Aug 1973 in Garland Cemetery, Annona,
Texas
Cause Of Death: Acute Myocardial Infarction
Occupation: Banker
Occupation: Welfare Agent
Military Service: SSgt., United States army

Joseph Dellinger Garland and Mary Julia Haney had the following children:

    i. SYLVIA ESTELLE[8] GARLAND was born on 24 Mar 1945 in Goose Creek, Texas. She married Joseph Theodore Leeds on 24 Nov 1966 in Clarkesville, Texas. He was born on 16 Sep 1942.

ii.   JUDY FRANCES GARLAND was born on 20 Mar 1948 in Roscoe, Texas. She died on 11 Feb 1993 in Dallas, Texas.

More About Judy Frances Garland:
Burial: 14 Feb 1993 in Garland Cemetery, Red River County, Texas

iii.   LILLIAN ELIZABETH GARLAND was born on 26 Nov 1951. She married Michael J. Lyons on 29 Oct 1982 in Dallas, Texas. He was born on 09 Oct 1942 in Little Rock, Arkansas.

NOTES;

Descendants of Francis Bullock

Generation 1

1.   **FRANCIS[1] BULLOCK** was born in 1767 in Bristol, England. He died in 1812 in Russellville, Franklin County, Alabama. He married **RACHEL VESTAL**. She was born in 1769 in Chatham, North Carolina. She died on 29 Feb 1844 in Russellville, Franklin County, Alabama.

Francis Bullock and Rachel Vestal had the following children:

2.   i. MARTHA JANE[2] BULLOCK was born about 1806 in North Carolina. She died on 01 Mar 1875 in Tishomingo County, Mississippi. She married (1) EDWARD GARLAND, son of Peter Garland and Mary Reamey about 1837 in Tennessee. He was born before 1807 in Henry County, Virginia. He died before 05 Dec 1850. She married
     ii. JONATHAN WINCHESTER, son of David Winchester and Zila Reves on 23 Dec 1867. He was born on 13 Dec 1798 in Rockingham, North Carolina. He died on 16 Dec 1873 in Tishomingo County, Mississippi.

3.   ii. WILLIAM JAMES BULLOCK was born about 1810 in North Carolina. He married ELIZABETH (UNKNOWN). She was born on 07 Oct 1811 in North Carolina. She died in 1880 in Russellville, Franklin County, Alabama.

Generation 2

2.   **MARTHA JANE[2] BULLOCK** (Francis[1]) was born about 1806 in North Carolina. She died on 01 Mar 1875 in Tishomingo County, Mississippi. She married (1) **EDWARD GARLAND**, son of Peter Garland and Mary Reamey about 1837 in Tennessee. He was born before 1807 in Henry County, Virginia. He died before 05 Dec 1850. She married (2) **JONATHAN WINCHESTER**, son of David Winchester and Zila Reves on 23 Dec 1867. He was born on 13 Dec 1798 in Rockingham, North Carolina. He died on 16 Dec 1873 in Tishomingo County, Mississippi.

More About Martha Jane Bullock:
Living In: 1855 Franklin County, Alabama
Living In: 1860 Franklin County, Alabama
Living In: 1870 Tishomingo County, Mississippi with her husband, Jonathan Winchester
Occupation: 1850 in Franklin County, Alabama; Farmer

Edward Garland and Martha Jane Bullock had the following children:

1.   ROBERT W.[3] GARLAND was born about 1838 in Alabama. He died on 31 Dec 1862 in Murfreesboro, Tennessee.

More About Robert W. Garland:
Living In: 1860 Living in the household of his mother in Franklin County, Alabama.
Occupation: 1860 in Franklin County, Alabama; Farmer
Military Service: Bet. 15 Jul 1861-31 Dec 1862; Company H, 16th Alabama Infantry, C.S.A.

Notes for Robert W. Garland:
Enlisted in Company H, 16th Alabama Infantry on July 15, 1861 at Tuscumbia, Colbert County, Alabama.
Killed in action December 31, 1862 at Murfreesboro, Tennessee.

2.   JOHN J. GARLAND was born about 1841 in Alabama.

More About John J. Garland:

Living In: 1860 With his uncle, William Bullock, in Franklin County, Alabama
Occupation: 1860 in Franklin County, Alabama; Farm Labor

4.   iii. RACHEL ANN GARLAND was born on 04 Oct 1844 in Henderson County, Tennessee. She died on 23 Aug 1929 in Franklin County, Alabama. She married Richard L. Winchester, son of Jonathan Winchester and Sarah Bruzil on 10 Feb 1867 in Pleasant Site, Franklin County, Alabama. He was born on 17 Feb 1839 in Heard County, Georgia. He died on 30 Jun 1919 in Pleasant Site, Franklin County, Alabama.

5.   iv. MARTHA ANN GARLAND was born on 29 Sep 1849 in Mississippi. She died on 08 Jan 1877 in Tishomingo County, Mississippi. She married Francis Marion Winchester, son of Jonathan Winchester and Ellenor Glover in Oct 1869. He was born in Jun 1849 in Mississippi. He died after 28 Apr 1910 in Texas.

More About Jonathan Winchester:
Living In: 1850 Living with his mother in Heard County, Georgia
Occupation: 1850 in Heard County, Georgia; Farmer
Occupation: 1860 in Marshall County, Alabama; Farmer
Occupation: 1870 in Tishomingo County, Mississippi; Farmer

3. **WILLIAM JAMES^2 BULLOCK** (Francis^1) was born about 1810 in North Carolina. He married **ELIZABETH (UNKNOWN)**. She was born on 07 Oct 1811 in North Carolina. She died in 1880 in Russellville, Franklin County, Alabama.

More About William James Bullock:
Occupation: 1860 in Franklin County, Alabama; Farmer

William James Bullock and Elizabeth (unknown) had the following children:

1. FRANKLIN^3 BULLOCK was born about 1834 in Alabama.

2. JOHN JAMES BULLOCK was born about 1834 in Alabama.

3. DORETHA JAMES BULLOCK was born about 1849 in Alabama.

Generation 3

4. **RACHEL ANN^3 GARLAND** (Martha Jane^2 Bullock, Francis^1 Bullock) was born on 04 Oct 1844 in Henderson County, Tennessee. She died on 23 Aug 1929 in Franklin County, Alabama. She married Richard L. Winchester, son of Jonathan Winchester and Sarah Bruzil on 10 Feb 1867 in Pleasant Site, Franklin County, Alabama. He was born on 17 Feb 1839 in Heard County, Georgia. He died on 30 Jun 1919 in Pleasant Site, Franklin County, Alabama.

More About Rachel Ann Garland:
Burial: 24 Aug 1929 in Winchester Cemetery, Franklin County, Alabama
Living In: 1860 With her uncle, William Bullock, in Franklin County, Alabama

Notes for Rachel Ann Garland:
Headstone has first name spelled as Rachel.

More About Richard L. Winchester:
Burial: Winchester Cemetery, Franklin County, Alabama
Occupation: 1870 in Franklin County, Alabama; Farmer

Occupation: 1880 in Franklin County, Alabama; Farmer
Occupation: 1900 in Pleasant Site, Franklin County, Alabama; Farmer
Occupation: 1910 in Burleson, Franklin County, Alabama; Retired
Military Service: Bet. 06 Sep 1862-13 Apr 1863; Company I, 4th Alabama Cavalry, C.S.A.

Notes for Richard L. Winchester:
Enlisted on September 6, 1862 in Marshall County, Alabama and mustered in to 4th
Alabama Cavalry on September 22, 1862.
Discharged for disability from 4th Alabama Cavalry on April 13, 1863 at Chattanooga, Tennessee.

Richard L. Winchester and Rachel Ann Garland had the following children:

> i. MARY LILLIE[4] WINCHESTER was born on 12 Nov 1868 in Russellville, Alabama. She died on 29 Dec 1935 in Belmont, Tishomingo County, Mississippi.

> JOHN J. WINCHESTER was born on 12 Jan 1869 in Franklin County, Alabama. He died on 20 Apr 1957 in Franklin County, Alabama.

> EDWARD B. WINCHESTER was born on 03 Mar 1871 in Alabama. He died on 26 Apr 1940.

> More About Edward B. Winchester:
> Burial: Winchester Cemetery, Franklin County, Alabama

> ALBERT C. WINCHESTER was born about 1874 in Alabama.

> HENRY J. WINCHESTER was born about 1878 in Alabama.

> ALTA WINCHESTER was born in Jun 1882 in Alabama.

> OCTAVUS G. WINCHESTER was born on 14 Oct 1885 in Alabama. He died on 20 Nov 1952.

> More About Octavus G. Winchester:
> Burial: Winchester Cemetery, Franklin County, Alabama

5. **MARTHA ANN**[3] **GARLAND** (Martha Jane[2] Bullock, Francis[1] Bullock) was born on 29 Sep 1849 in Mississippi. She died on 08 Jan 1877 in Tishomingo County, Mississippi. She married Francis Marion Winchester, son of Jonathan Winchester and Ellenor Glover in Oct 1869. He was born in Jun 1849 in Mississippi. He died after 28 Apr 1910 in Texas.

More About Martha Ann Garland:
Burial: Winchester Cemetery, Franklin County, Alabama

More About Francis Marion
Winchester:
Occupation: 1870 in Tishomingo County, Mississippi;
Farmer
Occupation: 1880 in Franklin County, Alabama; Farmer
Occupation: 1900 in Haskell County, Texas; Farmer
Occupation: 1910 in Weinert, Haskell County, Texas; Retired Farmer

Francis Marion Winchester and Martha Ann Garland had the following children:

1.   CHARLES WALTER[4] WINCHESTER was born on 13 Mar 1876 in Alabama. He died on 21 Mar 1959 in Wellington, Collingsworth County, Texas.

More About Charles Walter Winchester:
Burial: Johnson Cemetery, Munday, Texas
Occupation: Farmer

Notes for Charles Walter Winchester:
Birth date is from World War One draft registration.

ii.   LEE WINCHESTER.

iii.   CLARENCE WINCHESTER.

Descendants of Thomas Reamey

Generation 1

2.   **THOMAS[1] REAMEY** was born in 1724. He died in 1787 in Virginia. He married **MARY (UNKNOWN)**.

Thomas Reamey and Mary (unknown) had the following children:

2.   i. **DANIEL[2] REAMEY** was born in 1743 in Prince William County, Virginia. He died about 1803 in Henry County, Virginia. He married MARY (UNKNOWN). She died in 1826 in Henry County, Virginia.

      ii. ELIZABETH REAMEY was born on 05 Feb 1755 in Prince William County, Virginia. She died on 22 Apr 1855 in Henry County, Virginia. She married BENJAMIN JONES.

      iii. NANCY REAMEY.

Generation 2

2.   **DANIEL[2] REAMEY** (Thomas[1]) was born in 1743 in Prince William County, Virginia. He died about 1803 in Henry County, Virginia. He married **MARY (UNKNOWN)**. She died in 1826 in Henry County, Virginia.

Notes for Daniel Reamey:

Lived in Henry County, Virginia.

Daniel Reamey and Mary (unknown) had the following children:

3.   i. MARY[3] REAMEY. She died between 29 Nov 1843-07 Dec 1846 in Chester County, Tennessee. She married (1) PETER GARLAND, son of Peter Garland and Martha Garland before 1800. He was born about 1774 in Lunenburg County, Virginia. He died between 09 Oct 1817-03 Nov 1818 in Giles County, Tennessee. She married (2) THOMAS ALEXANDER, son of John Alexander and Nancy Nunn in Henry County, Virginia. He died in 1841 in Cumberland County, Kentucky.

WILLIAM WHALEY REAMEY.

JOHN REAMEY. He died in Irisburg, Virginia. He married (UNKNOWN) PACE. She died in Irisburg, Virginia.

DANIEL REAMEY. He married Susan Lynne Starling on 11 Aug 1825.

RAMATH REAMEY. She married Peyton Hunter on 08 Aug 1804.

JEMIMA REAMEY. She died in 1849 in Patrick County, Virginia. She married Terry Hughes on 01 Nov 1796.

LETICIA LETTY RAMEY. She married Micajah Hughes on 25 Jan 1802.

NANCY REAMEY. She married (UNKNOWN) ROWLAND.

ELIZABETH REAMEY.

Generation 3

3.   **MARY[3] REAMEY** (Daniel[2], Thomas[1]). She died between 29 Nov 1843-07 Dec 1846 in Chester County, Tennessee. She married (1) **PETER GARLAND**, son of Peter Garland and Martha Garland before 1800. He was born about 1774 in Lunenburg County, Virginia. He died between 09 Oct

1817-03 Nov 1818 in Giles County, Tennessee. She married (2) **THOMAS ALEXANDER**, son of John Alexander and Nancy Nunn in Henry County, Virginia. He died in 1841 in Cumberland County, Kentucky.

Notes for Mary Reamey:

Will Of Mary Reamey

I Mary Alexander do make and publish this as my last will and Testament hereby revoking and making void all other wills by me at any time made First I direct that my Funeral Expenses and all my debts be paid out of the first moneys that may come in to the hands of my Executor Secondly I give and bequeth unto my son Martin Alexander five dollars Thirdly I give and bequeth unto Greenwood Alexander five dollars   Fourthly I give and bequeth unto Nancy Pace five dollars Fifthly to my son Robert Garland five dollars Sixthly I give unto the heirs of my son Edward Garland five dollars Seventhly I give unto my daughter Francis Pate five dollars Eighthly I give unto my daughter Mary Angus five dollars Ninethly I give and bequeth unto my son Bonapart Garland a certain negroman slave named Joseph Tenthly the balance of all of my Estate to be Equally divided between my sons Bonapart Garland and Peter Garland and Thomas L. Garland and Harriet Wilmot Simmons and John C. Garland and William W. Garland I do hereby nominate and appoint my son William W. Garland as my Executor in witness where of I do to this my will set my hand and seal this the 29th november 1843.

(signed) Mary Alexander

Signed Sealed and published in our presance and we have subscribed our names hereto in the presance of the Testator

John C. Vantrease
William C. Vantrease

Will dated November 29, 1843
Will probated December 7, 1846

Autobiography of Joseph Daniel Garland, her grandson, states Mary is buried in Old Pisgah Cemetery, Chester County, Tennessee.

More About Peter Garland:
Military Service: War of 1812 - Virginia

Notes for Peter Garland:
Will dated October 9, 1817.
Will Proven November 3, 1818.
Inventory of Estate taken on November 12, 1818

Will Of Peter Garland

God have mercy on me and in his name I make and ordain this my last will and testament revoking all others I will one third part of all my Estate to my dear Wife and give her all my household and kitchen furniture during her natural life then to be divided between her two daughters Juliana and Maria Luisa The balance of my Estate I wish equally divided between the before mentioned two children and Mrs Alexanders children from Bonaparte Jefferson to Wirter Walt (torn off) all to have an equal proportion -Amen

9th Oct 1817   (signed) P Garland

Peter Garland and Mary Reamey had the following children:

i. MARY C. [4] GARLAND was born about 1795 in Virginia. She died between 09 Jul 1860-18 Aug 1870. She married Alexander Angus in Giles County, Tennessee. He was born about 1791 in Virginia. He died after 18 Aug 1870.

Notes for Mary C. Garland:
Possibly a daughter of Thomas Alexander who stayed with her mother when Thomas went to Kentucky.

ii. FRANCES GARLAND was born about 1797 in Henry County, Virginia. She married JOHN PATE.

Notes for Frances Garland:
Possibly a daughter of Thomas Alexander who stayed with her mother when Thomas went to Kentucky.

iii. BONAPARTE ROBERT GARLAND was born in 1801 in Henry County, Virginia. He died on 16 Aug 1884 in Franklin County, Alabama. He married Amanda W. Gardner, daughter of Theophilus Gardner and Elizabeth (unknown) on 24 Jan 1869 in Tishomingo County, Mississippi. She was born on 24 Jun 1824 in North Carolina. She died on 16 Feb 1901 in Mississippi.

More About Bonaparte Robert Garland:
Burial: Winchester Cemetery, Franklin County, Alabama
Living In: 1850 Living in the household of Joseph Bell in District 6, Franklin County, Alabama
Living In: 1859 Franklin County, Alabama
Occupation: Bet. 1828-1832 ; Justice of the Peace in Franklin County, Alabama
Occupation: Bet. 1842-1843 ; State Representative from Franklin County, Alabama
Occupation: Bet. 1845-1846 ; State Representative from Tuscaloosa, Alabama
Occupation: Bet. 1847-1848 ; State Representative from Franklin County, Alabama
Occupation: 1850 in District 6, Franklin County, Alabama; Farmer
Occupation: 1870 in Township 6, Range 15, Franklin County, Alabama; Farmer
Occupation: 1880 in Franklin County, Alabama; Farmer
Property: 01 Dec 1859 in Purchased Land Offered for Sale by U.S. Government at Huntsville, Alabama; 79 and 87/100 Acres
Property: 1880 in Franklin County, Alabama; 320 Acres (20 tilled and 300 woodland)

iv. DANIEL REAMEY GARLAND was born about 1802 in Henry County, Virginia. He died before 1841.
More About Daniel Reamey Garland:
Living In: 06 Oct 1840 Franklin County, Alabama
Property: 06 Oct 1840; Purchased land offered for sale by the U.S. Government at Pontotoc, Mississippi: 160 and 80/100 Acres
Property: 06 Oct 1840; Purchased land offered for sale by the U.S. Government at Pontotoc, Mississippi: 160 Acres

v. ROBERT REAMEY GARLAND was born about 1804 in Henry County, Virginia. He died in Vicksburg, Mississippi.

vi. PETER GARLAND was born on 30 Dec 1805 in Henry County, Virginia. He died on 24

Feb 1873 in Thorp Spring, Hood County, Texas. He married (1) Lucinda A . Goff, daughter of Thomas Goff and (unknown) Allen before 1831 in Tennessee. She was born in Tennessee. She died in Mississippi. He married (2) Louisa Phillips in 1845 in Curdy, Mississippi. She was born on 08 Feb 1828 in Mississippi. She died on 31 Dec 1902 in Chickasha, Chickasha Nation, Indian Territory (present day Oklahoma).

More About Peter Garland:
Burial: Thorp Spring Cemetery, Thorp Spring, Texas
Living In: 1840 Tishomingo County, Mississippi
Living In: 1841 Tishomingo County, Mississippi
Living In: 1845 Tishomingo County, Mississippi
Occupation: Bet. 1842-1843 ; Deputy Sheriff, Tishomingo County, Mississippi
Occupation: 1850 in Northern Division District 4, Tishomingo County, Mississippi; Farmer
Occupation: 1870 in Hood County, Texas; Farmer
Property: 06 Feb 1860 in Houston and Nacogdoches Land Districts, Henderson County, Texas; With his son, Christopher, purchased 80 acres.
Property: 1869 in Erath County, Texas; With his son, C.C. Garland, 640 Acres. Property: 21 Dec 1870 in Milam District, Erath County, Texas; With his son, Christopher, purchased 80 acres.

Notes for Peter Garland:

CAPTAIN PETER GARLAND.

FRONTIERSMAN.

by Barbara Thorp Wilkins

Peter and Louisa (Phillips) Garland moved from near Stephenville in Erath County to Hood County in 1860, settling on Stroud's Creek near Thorp Spring. As the Civil War loomed, bloody Comanche raids on the settlers of the frontier area continued and would for another decade, despite removal of all Indian tribes from northern Texas to the reservations of what is now Oklahoma.

Controversy followed the volatile Garland to Hood County, and some historical writers still debate the part he played in the early history of this "wide-open" part of Texas. As a Captain in the Frontier Guard, Garland has alternately been condemned as an "Indian-hater of the first order" and "murderer" and hailed as a fearless Indian fighter, defender of the frontier, leading citizen and hero. In retrospect, out of the context of the times, it is doubtful that controversy will ever be resolved. In his Hood County History, Thomas Ewell commented that Garland was "honored and trusted by the people who knew him best and were personally cognizant of all the events." This must have reflected the views of many of Garland's contemporaries, as he was elected the first Treasurer of Hood County in 1867.

Capt. Peter Garland of Texas was born in 1805 in Henry County, Virginia, the grandson of Col. David Garland of the Revolution and son of Maj. Peter Garland of the Virginia 64th Regiment in the War of 1812. His grandfather and father had wars to fight. Capt. Peter Garland, some say, created his own war, against the Indians of the Texas frontier..

After leaving Virginia, young Garland was first married to Lucinda Goff in Tennessee and second to Louisa Phillips in Mississippi as he traveled the migration route to Texas, fathering a total of at least 12 children. Before coming to Anderson County, Texas, in 1850, Garland was a Deputy Sheriff, Circuit Court Clerk and saloonkeeper in Tishomingo County, Mississippi. In 1857, the Garlands braved the raw frontier of Erath County along with several other families, including the Thorntons, Hightowers and Wylies. Ten years later, in Hood County, Peter and Louisa's 16-year-old daughter, Melissa Virginia, was married to James Goodhope Thorp, eldest son of Pleasant and Nancy Thorp, founders of Thorp Spring. James and Melissa Virginia had nine children, all born in Thorp Spring; and their fourth child was Pleasant Garland Thorp, my grandfather..

Capt. Peter Garland died in 1873 in Thorp Spring and is buried there in the old Thorp Spring Cemetery..

This article was scanned from the Hood County Genealogical Society Newsletter No. 16, dated November 1987, Editor Merle McNeese

----

7.   EDWARD GARLAND was born before 1807 in Henry County, Virginia. He died before Dec 1850. He married (1) NANCY W. SMISER, daughter of John Smiser and Eve Mary Turney on 14 May 1821 in Columbia, Tennessee. She was born about 1805 in Maury County, Tennessee. She died before 1840. He married (2) MARTHA JANE BULLOCK, daughter of Francis Bullock and Rachel Vestal about 1837 in Tennessee. She was born about 1806 in North Carolina. She died on 01 Mar 1875 in Tishomingo County, Mississippi.

8.   THOMAS LOWERY GARLAND was born on 20 Jul 1807 in Henry County, Virginia. He died on 24 Sep 1868 in White County, Arkansas. He married Saphronia Richardson Hearn, daughter of Isham Green Hearn and Amy Gilliam Harris in 1827 in Madison County, Tennessee. She was born on 15 Jun 1812 in North Carolina. She died on 22 Jul 1858 in Chester County, Tennessee.

More About Thomas Lowery Garland:
Burial: Old Pisgah Cemetery, Chester County, Tennessee
Living In: 01 May 1861 White County, Arkansas
Occupation: 1850 in Madison County, Tennessee; Farmer
Occupation: 1860 in near Bradford, White County, Arkansas; Farmer
Occupation: Methodist Minister
Property: 01 May 1861; Purchased 80 acres from land offered for sale by U.S. Government at Batesville, Arkansas.

Notes for Thomas Lowery Garland:
Autobiography of Joseph D. Garland gives birthdate as April 20, 1807. Headstone shows July 20, 1807. Autobiography gives death date as September 20, 1868. Headstone gives death date as September 24, 1868.

ix.   HARRIET WILMOT GARLAND was born on 04 Jul 1810 in Henry County, Virginia. She died on 15 Jul 1859 in Chester County, Tennessee. She married James Martin Simmons, son of Solomon Simmons and Mary (unknown) about 1827 in Giles County, Tennessee. He was born about 1801 in Wake County, North Carolina. He died after 10 Jun 1880.

More About Harriet Wilmot Garland:
Burial: Old Pisgah Cemetery, Chester County, Tennessee
Living In: 1850 District 1, Madison County, Tennessee with her children.

Notes for Harriet Wilmot Garland:
Will probated September 1, 1859 in Madison County, Tennessee.

10.   JOHN CALHOUN GARLAND was born on 12 Dec 1810 in Henry County, Virginia. He
      died on 02 Sep 1874 in Annona, Texas. He married Nancy Johnson, daughter of
      Joseph Johnson and (unknown) about 1839 in Montgomery, Tennessee. She
      was born on 30 May 1815 in North Carolina. She died on 30 Nov 1881 in
      Annona, Texas. He met (UNKNOWN) GARLAND.

      More About John Calhoun Garland: Burial:
      Garland Cemetery, Annona, Texas
      Occupation: 1850 in disrict 3, McNairy County, Tennessee; Farmer
      Occupation: 1860 in Beat 3, Bowie County, Texas; Farmer
      Occupation: 1870 in Precinct 3, Red River County, Texas; Farmer
      Property: 1870 in Red River County, Texas; 240 Acres Improved and 4300
      Acres Unimproved

11.   WILLIAM WIRT GARLAND was born on 15 Aug 1812 in Henry County, Virginia. He
      died on 06 Jun 1901 in Madison County, Tennessee. He married Elizabeth A.
      Exum, daughter of John Exum and Martha (unknown) on 15 Jan 1841 in
      Madison County, Tennessee. She was born in 1818 in Tennessee. She died in
      1873 in Tennessee.

      More About William Wirt Garland:
      Occupation: 1850 in Madison County, Tennessee; Farmer
      Occupation: 1860 in Madison County, Tennessee; Farmer
      Occupation: 1870 in Madison County, Tennessee; Farmer
      Occupation: 1880 in Madison County, Tennessee; Farmer
      Occupation: 1900 in Chester County, Tennessee; Farmer
      Property: 1850 in Madison County, Tennessee; 200 Acres Improved and 900
      Acres Unimproved
      Property: 1870 in Madison County, Tennessee; 150 Acres Improved and 700
      Acres Unimproved
      Property: 1880 in Madison County, Tennessee; 300 Acres Improved and 840
      Acres Unimproved

Notes for Thomas Alexander:
Will Dated August 25, 1837.
Will Codicil dated December 16,
1840. Will Proved October 6, 1841.
                    Thomas Alexander
   Decd. In the name of God amen.
   I Thomas Alexander of the County of Cumberland and the State of Kentucky being in
perfect mind and Memory, do make this my last Will and Testament hereby Revoking,
Annuling, and Making Void, all and every other Will and Testament by me made - In manner
and form following (viz.)
   1st

It is my will that all the perishable part of my property be sold immediately after my death and out of the moneys arising therefrom my Executors to pay all my just debts and funeral expenses, and if the same should not produce funds sufficient for the aforesaid purposes. Then I hereby authorise my Executors to dispose of such other of my Estate as they may think proper. Not interfering with specified legacies and devices, and from such monies therefrom arising to satisfy all my Creditors that shall remain unpaid after the perishable part of my estate as heretofore devised shall be paid or appropriated.

2nd

I give to my John M Alexander Jr one negro girl Lucy and her future increase one Feather Bed and Furniture, and Ninety dollars in Money.

3rd

I give to my son Greenwood Alexander one negro girl Jimmey and her future increase, one feather bed and furniture and $90 in money.

4th

I give to my daughter Nancy Pace wife of John Pace decd one negro girl Polly and her future increase, one feather bed and furniture and $90 in money.

5th

I give to my daughter Susanah Gearhart one negro girl named Polly which was bequeathed to me by my Father one feather bed furniture and $90 in money.

6th

I give to my son Philip N. Alexander one negro boy named Frank, one Feather bed and furniture and $90 in money.

7th

I give to my wife Nancy Alexander one negro boy Ma?? one feather bed and furniture and $90 in money, during her natural life and at her death to be disposed of by her in any way she may think proper.

8th

I give to Polly Alexander (alias) Garland, to Francis Alexander (alias) Garland to Robert Alexander (alias) Garland, to Edward Alexander (alias) Garland, to Buonapart Alexander (alias) Garland, to Peter Alexander (alias) Garland Thomas Alexander (alias) Garland, to Harriet Alexander (alias) Garland, John Alexander (alias) Garland and Wa??a? Wa???? Alexander (alias) Garland each one dollar and no more, they being the children of my former wife Polly Alexander.

9th

My plantation whereon I now live I wish my son Philip Alexander to take at my death as $?00 provided he may think proper to do so, the price to be deducted from his part of said legacy and should there not be that amount coming to him to have one and two years to pay the balance, and provided my son Philip N. Alexander should not think proper to take the land at the price specified, in that case it my wish that my wife Nancy Alexander have the benifit of the Land during her natural life and at her death to be sold by my executors as Such Terms as they may think proper and the proceeds together with all the residue of my Estate after paying all my debts, and satisfying the foregoing bequeaths to be sold and equally divided amongst my children John M. Alexander Jr. Greenwood Alexander, Nancy Pace, Susanah Gearhart & Philip N. Alexander, and I do hereby appoint Reubin Alexander and John Dabny Alexander my executors of this my Last Will and Testament.

In Testimony Whereof I have hereto set my hand and seal this 25th of August 1837

(signed)   Thomas Alexander

Attest
William N. Alexander
John E. Alexander
Martha S. Alexander

Codicil

I Thomas Alexander of Cumberland County and State of Kentucky do hereby make and publish this Codicil to be added to my Will and Testament in manner and form following (to wit) I give and bequeath to my wife Nancy Alexander during her natural life one negro Woman Amy, one Horse worth $60.00 one cow & calf and provision sufficient to Last her one year, & at her death the negro Woman Amy to be sold and equally divided among the foregoing Legatees mentiond in this will as other property, and lastly it is my will and desire that this my present Codicil be ammended to a made a part of my last Will and Testament aforesaid.
Witness hereof to have hereunto set my hand and seal this 16th day of Dec. 1840.

(signed) Thomas Alexander

attest
John E. Alexander
William N. Alexander

State of Kentucky
Cumberland County viz.
I John Adams King a Deputy Clerk of the County Court for the County afod. do certify that the Within Will of Thomas Alexander deceased was produced in open Court at the September Term 1841 and was proven by the oath of William N. Alexander and of the subscribing witnesses thereto and the same is ordered to record, which is truly recorded in my said office in Will book D page 100.
Witness my hand this 6th day of October 1841

(signed) John A. King C. Clk

Thomas Alexander and Mary Reamey had the following children:

i. JOHN MARTIN[4] ALEXANDER was born in 1789 in Virginia.

ii. GREENWOOD ALEXANDER was born in 1790 in Virginia. He married ELIZABETH SMILEY. She was born in 1792 in Cumberland County, Kentucky.

 Notes for Greenwood Alexander:
 Served in War of 1812

iii. NANCY ALEXANDER was born on 13 Mar 1793 in Virginia. She married JOHN MARTIN PACE. He was born on 01 Jan 1787 in Henry County, Virginia.

www.ingramcontent.com/pod-product-compliance
Lightning Source LLC
Chambersburg PA
CBHW080818280726
48660CB00018B/3511